VIKING GODS

Liina Maialle
Jouluna 2002
Juluilon ja
Onnellista Uutta Vuotta 2003
Seis - ukki (grandpa)
Anja - mummi (grandma)
Merry Christmas and Happy New Year 2003

VIKING GODS

Grange
BOOKS

A QUANTUM BOOK

Published by Grange Books
an imprint of Grange Books Plc
The Grange
Kingsnorth Industrial Estate
Hoo, nr. Rochester
Kent ME3 9ND

1-84013-118-7

This book is produced by
Quantum Books Ltd
6 Blundell Street
London N7 9BH

Project Manager: Rebecca Kingsley
Project Editor: Judith Millidge
Designer: Wayne Humphries
Editor: Clare Haworth-Maden

The material in this publication previously appeared in
Viking Mythology

QUMVKGD
Set in Times
Reproduced in Singapore by Eray Scan
Printed in Singapore by Star Standard Industries (Pte) Ltd

CONTENTS

The beginning and the end   6

Viking gods   17

Viking goddesses   33

A glossary of gods and
goddesses   49

THE BEGINNING
AND
THE END

The Vikings were a Teutonic people who established themselves in Scandinavia between the late eighth century and the middle of the eleventh century. Viking mythology is Norse mythology, and Norse mythology is in turn the best recorded version of Teutonic mythology. Viking mythology includes an elaborate creation myth, as well as a graphic description of the future ending of the world, at Ragnarok.

Above: A reconstruction of a Viking farm at Stong, Iceland.

THE CREATION

In the beginning there was nothing. No, not quite nothing. There was an endless space and a god called Allfather who was invisible and who had existed forever. He had eleven other names, ranging from Spearshaker to Gelding to Ruler of Weather. The abyss of emptiness was called Ginnungagap. Long before the Earth was created, there came to exist Yggdrasil, the World Tree, an ash that would link all of the nine worlds.

Under one of its roots, to the south, there was a realm called Muspell, which was so hot that anyone who did not live there would be

Opposite: A reconstruction of a Viking helmet found at Middleton Cross, Yorkshire, England.

Above: Surtr, the giant with the flaming sword who guarded the realm of Muspell, or the 'Home of Brightness. It was also the home of the sons of Muspel the fire giant.

consumed by the heat; it was guarded by a giant called Surtr who was armed with a burning sword. This was a place of fire: embers from it floated down into Ginnungagap. Under another root, to the north, there was a realm called Niflheim, a land of mist and darkness; directly beneath this great root was Hvergelmir, a bubbling cauldron that supplied the waters for twelve huge rivers. In the cauldron there was also a repellent dragon called Nidhug that gnawed away at the roots of the great tree; when it and its worm-like allies succeed in killing the tree, the world will come to an end. The waters of the rivers pouring from Hvergelmir flowed torrentially into Ginnungagap and, as they fell into the frigid void, became great blocks of ice.

THE INCARNATION OF YMIR

Far down, at the base of Ginnungagap, the embers from Muspell dropped onto these piles of ice so that great clouds of steam arose. The steam turned into rime, which progressively filled up Ginnungagap. To the north, near Niflheim, there were gales and also a never-ending drizzle of cold rain; to the south, near Muspell, the glowing embers lit up the sky as they met the ascending rime. The result was that the centre of the rising surface became a temperate ocean. This was incarnated in the form of an evil giant called Ymir – the first of the ice giants.

YMIR AND BURI

The thawing of the rime also created a cow, Audhumla. Her udder gave out four streams of milk, and from these Ymir was able to gain sustenance. The cow licked blocks of salty ice so that, on the first day, the hair of a being appeared; her licking on the second day revealed the head of the being; her licking on

the third exposed the entire body of this being, Buri. In the meantime, Ymir had been sleeping, and as he slept he sweated; from the sweat of his left armpit, some say, were born the first man and the first woman. Ymir's legs copulated with each other to produce a six-headed giant called Thrudgelmir, who in due course gave birth to Bergelmir, the direct ancestor of the frost giants.

Buri became the forefather of the gods. He had a son, Börr, and the two of them immediately began to battle against the evil giants. The battle lasted for a longer time than human beings can reckon, but then Börr married a giantess called Bestla and sired three great sons: Odin, Vili and Ve. These three leapt into battle alongside their father, so that soon Ymir was slain. All the giants were drowned in the

Above: The 'Waterfall of the Gods' in Iceland. According to legend, Thorsten, on being converted to Christianity in about AD 1000, threw his pagan idols over these falls.

Right: A Danish bronze plaque of a horse, dating from about AD 400–800.

Below: An animal head, probably from the bow of a Viking longship, discovered in the River Scheldt, Belgium.

flood of Ymir's blood except Bergelmir and his mate; these two fled in a longship to a place called Jotunheim, where they bred. The frost giants who descended from Bergelmir and his wife perhaps understandably regarded the gods ever after as their natural foes – even though, on occasion, members of the two factions could exhibit amity.

ODIN, VILI AND VE

Odin, Vili and Ve were left with Ymir's corpse. They tugged it out across Ginnungagap and started to chop it up to make the various parts of the physical world. Our world of mortals, Midgard, they manufactured from Ymir's flesh; the giant's blood they used for oceans and his unbroken bones for the mountains. His broken bones, his teeth and bits of his jaw became the cliffs, rocks and stones of the world. His skull they made into the dome of the sky; to keep it aloft they created four dwarfs (Austri, Nordri, Sudri and Westri), corresponding to the four cardinal points, who supported it. His brains became the clouds. They then used the embers from Muspell to create the light that

illuminates both heaven and the Earth; they also made the stars and the planets.

THE SUN AND THE MOON

The brightest of the embers from Muspell were given special names and special prominence: they were the Moon (Mani) and the Sun (Sol). These two beings were set by the three gods into chariots that were designed to cross the sky. The two horses drawing Sol's chariot, Arvakr and Alsvin, had to be protected from Sol's great heat: they were endowed with cooling devices plus the shielding of another device called Svalin. The horse that drew Mani's chariot was called Alsvider. Mani had two attendants, children he snatched up from the ground while they were collecting water from a well. They were called Hiuki and Bil, and represented the waxing and waning Moon. Mani precedes Sol across the sky, but Sol is always in a hurry to catch up. This is because Sol is being pursued by a wolf called Sköll. Mani is likewise being chased by a wolf, Hati. From time to time the wolves succeed in catching their prey, so that the light of the

Moon or Sun is blotted out; however, people on Earth can make enough noise to scare the wolves away and restore the light. In the end, though – just before Ragnarok – the wolves will finally triumph.

GUARDIAN DEITIES

A giant called Norvi had a daughter called Nott, or Night. She, in turn, had children by three husbands: Aud was her son by her first husband, Naglfari; Fjorgyn (Jörd, 'Earth') was her daughter by her second husband, Annar; Dag ('day'), an astoundingly beautiful and radiant youth, was her son by her third husband, Dellinger, the god of dawn, a relation of Odin, Vili and Ve. These three gods gave Nott a chariot in which she could circle the heavens; it was drawn by a horse called Hrimfaxi. Later, when they saw the beauty of Dag, they gave him a chariot as well; its horse was Skinfaxi. The mane of Skinfaxi gives off a brilliant light which serves to illuminate the world.

THE REGULATORS OF TIME

The gods appointed various other guardians. The responsibility for the changing of the seasons was divided between Winter and Summer. Winter was the grandson of the god Vasud – the frigid wind – and the son of Vinsval. Winter took on their nastier characteristics and therefore unreasonably loathed Summer, who was the son of a benign and lovely god called Svasud. Less important guardians of the regularity of the passing of time were Noon, Afternoon, Evening, Midnight, Morning and Forenoon.

Right: A detail from a twelfth- or thirteenth-century wooden portal at Hylestad Church, Norway, showing the dwarf Regin reforging Sigurd's sword.

Above: Hjorleifshofdi, on the southern coast of Iceland, was the first Viking settlement on the island.

DWARFS AND FAIRIES

When Odin, Vili and Ve had been reducing Ymir's body to its constituent parts, they had noticed that the flesh of the giant's body had been crawling with maggots. They decided to be merciful to these creatures. They gave them a subhuman form, the nature of which depended upon their spiritual characteristics. Those whose ethics were questionable became dwarfs; they were condemned to live underground, knowing that if they came out into the open during the day they would instantly be turned into stone. (Dwarfs could also be called dark elves, gnomes, kobolds or trolls; whatever the name, they were banished to Svartalfaheim.) The maggots that were considered ideologically sound became fairies and elves. They were given the lovely realm of Alfheim, which was halfway between heaven and Earth; from here they could flit down to Earth whenever they wanted. Neither of these two classes of being could be considered human. Normally they were deadly enemies but on occasion they could be friendly towards mortals or gods.

ASGARD AND MIDGARD

The three gods then created the first human beings out of a pair of trees they discovered. Odin's contributions to these people were life and spirit, Vili's mobility and intelligence, and Ve's the senses. The first man was called Askr (meaning 'ash tree') and the first woman Embla (meaning, possibly, 'elm').

The gods next created their own realm, Asgard, and the realm of mortals, Midgard.

Mortals were unable to see Asgard because the plain on which it was sited, Idavold (or Idavoll), floated far above the Earth. A river called Ifing separated Idavold from the rest of the world; its waters never froze. However, there was a link between our mortal Earth and Asgard: the magical bridge called Bifrost, which was equated with the rainbow whose colours were born of fire, water and the air. The gods were able to use this bridge to travel up and down to Midgard. One difficulty that the gods faced was that their weight might shatter Bifrost; Thor therefore eschewed the bridge altogether, while the others trod warily. At the Midgard end of the bridge stood the god Heimdall clutching a horn. Every time the gods entered or left Asgard, Heimdall would sound a quiet note on this instrument.

YGGDRASIL

All of the worlds were still connected by the trunk of the great ash tree Yggdrasil, whose roots lay in Asgard, Jotunheim and Niflheim. Its topmost bough, Lerad, had perched on it an eagle between whose eyes sat a hawk called Vedfolnir; it was the duty of Vedfolnir to look down over all of heaven, Earth and Niflheim and report what was happening there. Yggdrasil had other infesting fauna. Aside from Nidhug, chewing at the tree's roots, there were the four deer – Dain, Duneyr, Durathor and Dvalin – that roamed among its branches; the dew dripping from their antlers came together to form the world's rivers. Then there was a squirrel called Ratatosk; it spent its time running up and down the great tree's trunk exchanging malicious gossip between the eagle and the dragon, hoping to make them declare war on each other. The Norns had the daily task of

Below: A ninth- or twelfth-century golden arm-ring from Rabylille, Denmark, decorated with symbols of Yggdrasil.

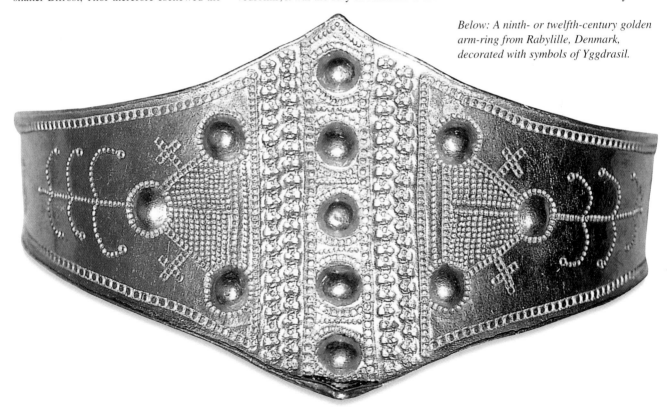

sprinkling water from a blessed well called Urdar down over the branches of Yggdrasil, so that the great tree was constantly refreshed; the water falling from the lower branches became bees' honey.

THE AESIR AND THE VANIR

The family of gods sired by Odin and his brothers was called the Aesir. But there was also another family of older gods, the Vanir, fertility gods whose powers were generally related to those of the wind and the sea; they lived in Vanaheim. Very early on there was a war between the Aesir and the Vanir. Because the result was a stalemate, so hostages were

Above: Part of a carved cross slab found at Jurby, Isle of Man, depicting Heimdall blowing his horn to summon the gods.

Right: At Ragnarok Thor will battle Jormungand; Odin will fight Fenris; and Frey will struggle with Surtr.

exchanged. The Vanir sent Njord to Asgard with his two children, Frey and Freya, and the Aesir sent Mimir and Hoenir, a brother of Odin, to Vanaheim. This disposition of gods seems to have suited everybody, because Frey and Freya became important members of the Norse pantheon, while Hoenir will be one of the very few lucky enough to survive Ragnarok.

RAGNAROK

Viking mythology also encompassed what was going to happen at some unspecified time in the future, when the gods themselves would die. Here there is a definite parallel with the Christian account, in Revelation, of the forthcoming Apocalypse, for Ragnarok too is a final battle between the forces of good and evil. (The German equivalent of Ragnarok is, of course, Götterdämmerung.) Ragnarok will be brought about largely because the gods tolerated the existence of the evil Loki, who, bound

in the most horrific circumstances, has long plotted their downfall.

The first sign of the onset of Ragnarok will be Fimbulvetr, a year's-long savage winter when snow will constantly fall from all points of the compass. The wolves chasing the Sun and the Moon will catch up with them and devour them. Loki and Fenris, as well as Hel's dog, Garm, will succeed in breaking their bonds in order to attack the gods. Nidhug, the dragon gnawing at one of the roots of Yggdrasil, will at last succeed in severing it. The god Heimdall will sound a note on his trumpet, warning of what is imminent, and this note will be heard by all. The Aesir and the Einheriar (the dead warriors taken to Valhalla from the battlefield) will hear this blast and rally to Vigrid, where the final battle will take place. The seas will be stirred up into a frenzy and this will trigger Jormungand, the World Serpent, into raising himself from

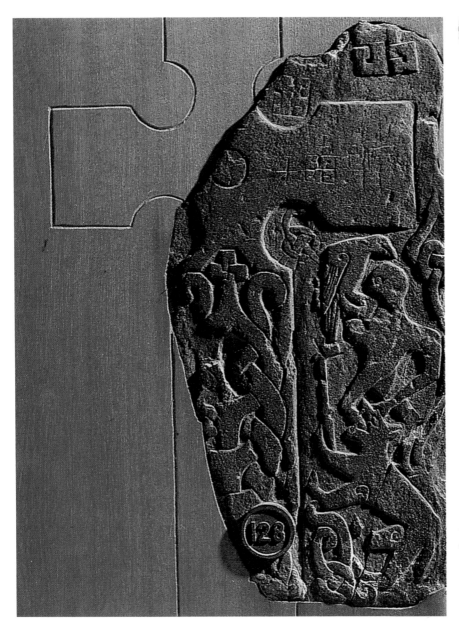

Above: A detail from a stone-carved cross from Middleton, North Yorkshire, showing a Norse warrior laid out for burial.

Left: Thorwald's Cross Slab, at Andreas, Isle of Man, shows Odin being attacked by Fenris at Ragnarok.

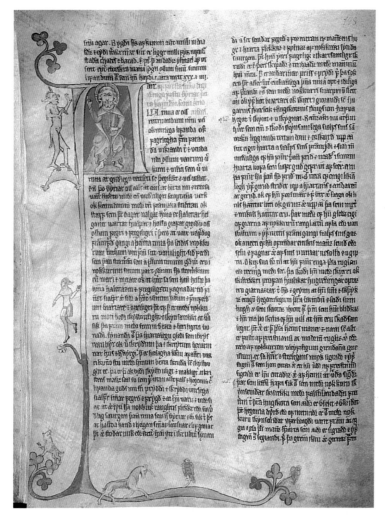

Above: Pages from a fourteenth-century Icelandic biblical text. Many Viking myths were modified to accommodate Christianity.

his bed in the depths of the ocean to join in the battle.

The serpent's writhing will create huge waves, and one of these will launch a ship called Naglfari, created entirely from the nails of those of the dead whose kin have failed to cut their nails. Loki will board this ship, accompanied by a horde from the realm of Muspell. The frost giants, too, will sail in a ship to Vigrid in order to battle with the Aesir; their captain will be the giant Hrym. Hel will join the forces of evil, as will her sycophants Garm and Nidhug. Surtr, the flame giant, will come to add to Loki's army, followed by numerous of his kin. As this vast army rides over Bifrost its sheer weight will shatter the rainbow bridge.

DEATH AND REBIRTH

The gods will show no fear despite the strength of the armies facing them. Odin will, one last time, consult the Norns and Mimir, and then rejoin his fellows. Then the battle will be joined. Odin will be slain in his duel with Fenris, Surtr will kill Frey and Loki Heimdall. Tyr will die at the teeth of Garm, and Thor in a torrent of venom from the mouth of Jormungand. Vidar will tear Fenris to pieces. Surtr will set fire to Yggdrasil, thereby destroying also the halls of the gods and all of the plant life of the Earth.

However, things will come into being again. A daughter of Sol will drive the chariot of the Sun, and will do so in much better fashion than her mother had done. The first two mortals of the new race after Ragnarok will be called Lif and Lifthrasir; they will repopulate the Earth with their children. The gods Vali and Vidar will survive the battle, as will the sons of Thor – Magni and Modi – and the god Hoenir. Balder and Hoder will also be returned to life.

Christianity made its mark on Norse mythology, too, and so it is recorded that, after Ragnarok, there will be the incarnation of a god too great to be named – in other words, Jahweh, or God.

VIKING
GODS

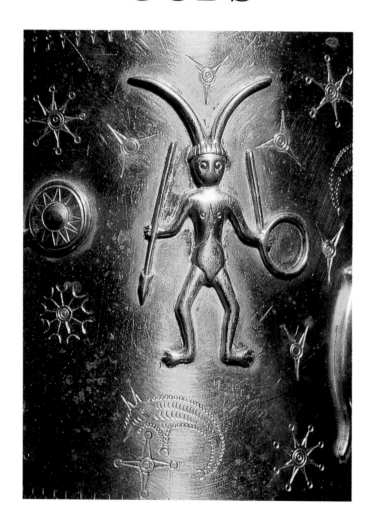

Below: An eighth-century Swedish stela from Tjängvide, showing Odin's eight-legged steed, Sleipnir.

This chapter provides a comprehensive introduction to four of the most important Viking gods: Odin, the leader of the gods, who was simultaneously wise, kind and cruel; Thor, the hammer-wielding, thunder-creating scourge of the giants; Frey, the Vanir god of fertility who was the subject of an extensive popular cult; and Loki, the trickster god whose mischief and malice caused the gods to bind him until he will finally break free and initiate the apocalyptic battle of Ragnarok.

ODIN

Odin is often called Allfather, which is the name of the primordial deity who initiated the creation; in fact, in many of the legends it is assumed that the two gods are one and the same. This may seem like an inconsistency in the mythology – and probably is – but we should remind ourselves that there is a parallel in Christianity, where Christ is both God and the son of God. A further resemblance to this situation is found in a legend relating how Odin, pierced by a spear, was hanged for nine days and nights from a branch of Yggdrasil as a sacrifice to himself. During this time he learned great wisdoms and invented the runes; he became the patron god of hanged men. There are many tales about Odin, and we shall look at only a few.

Odin required no food, although he would partake of the gods' heavenly mead. His spear was Gungnir, which always found its mark; in addition, it had the property that any oath sworn upon it could never be broken. He owned the magical golden ring called Draupnir; every night this would shed eight replicas of itself. His steed Sleipnir, a son of Loki, had eight legs and could travel at colossal speed all over the nine worlds.

Odin's halls were Gladsheim, Valaskialf and Valhalla. Valhalla was the hall of Odin to which the warriors slaughtered in battle – the

Einheriar – were brought so that they could enjoy a glorious afterlife. Each morning they had to dress in their armour and then do combat in the plain before Valhalla. Each evening they were brought back to life, free from any of the mutilations they might have suffered, and came back to Valhalla to engage in feats of consuming limitless food and mead. The boiled meat they ate came from a huge boar called Saehrimnir and the supplies were unending because even though the boar was slaughtered each day by Valhalla's cook, Andhrimnir, it would be reborn in time to be slaughtered again for their next meal. The mead came from the udder of Odin's goat Heidrun, who supplied more than enough for the Einheriar, who drank it from the skulls of their enemies. The servants at the gargantuan feasts were the Valkyries, sumptuous young women whose favours were available to the bold, although at the same time they remained everlastingly virginal.

ODIN THE ALL-KNOWING

Odin's high throne in Asgard was called Hlidskialf, and when seated on it Odin could see everything that happened anywhere; Frigga, his second wife, was also allowed to sit here (his other two wives were Jörd and Rind). Further information from the worlds was brought to him by his two ravens, Hugin and Munin, who flew from Asgard each morning and returned each evening. He was the master of two wolves, Freki and Geri, which he personally fed. He was one-eyed because he had drunk from the well of the wise god Mimir, and had willingly surrendered an eye for the continuing wisdom he received.

Right: The remains of a tenth-century Viking warrior, buried with his weaponry.

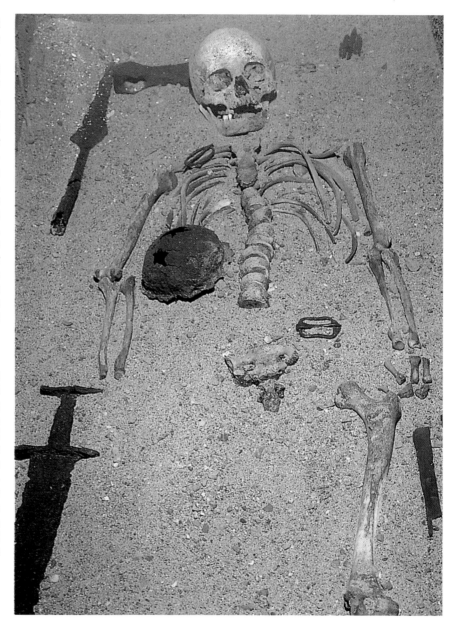

Above: Odin and a group of beautiful Valkyries welcome a dead hero to Valhalla; note the two ravens and pair of wolves.

Right: A stone from Lärbro, Sweden. In the central panel is depicted Odin's horse Sleipnir carrying a dead hero to Valhalla.

He was instrumental in starting the war between the Vanir and the Aesir. A witch called Gullveig – probably one of the Vanir – came to Asgard and explained to Odin that she was consumed by the lust for gold. The Aesir were revolted by her avariciousness and determined to put her to death; they tried this three times. The Aesir then gave up their attempts and the witch, now called Heid, was permitted to wander through Asgard. However, the Vanir were enraged when they heard how she had been treated and war began when Odin impatiently threw his great spear at the rallied Vanir.

THOR

Along with Odin and Loki, the god of thunder was among the most important in the Norse pantheon. He was responsible for weather and

Left: An Icelandic bronze statuette, dating from about the year 1000, showing Thor with his hammer.

Below: A tenth-century cross shaft from Sockburn, Country Durham, showing a mounted Odin with a raven on his shoulder.

crops, as well as for sea voyages that might be affected by the weather. Interestingly, the cracking of the sky during thunderstorms was not regarded with dread by the Norse people, but as a sign that Thor was carrying out his responsibilities, which were, essentially, the slaughter of giants.

Thor was red-bearded, gluttonous and loud-voiced; his standard way of dealing with any problem was to kill anyone foolish enough to be nearby. His invincible hammer was Miölnir and his wife was the beautiful goddess Sif. Thor, because of his violent encounter with the giant Hrungnir, will spend all of the rest of time until Ragnarok with a stone implanted in his head, the result of the giant's stone club being shattered by Miölnir during a duel.

THIALFI AND ROSKVA

Thor had two regular attendants: the boy Thialfi and a girl, Roskva. The god gained them in a rather despicable way. He and Loki were wandering the world when the two gods decided that they would like lodging for the night. They took this from a very poor peasant couple, who produced a supper that was in no way big enough to satisfy Thor's huge appetite. The god therefore killed their only two goats – although he told the family that, should they leave all the bones untouched and put them back into the empty skins of the animals, things would be all right in the morning.

LOKI'S TRICKERY

This would have been an honest enough scheme had not Loki encouraged the son of the house, Thialfi, to break one of the bones and lick out its marrow. The next day Thor

Left: Arthur Rackham's conception of Thor, an illustration for Wagner's Das Rheingold.

touched the two heaps of skin and bones with his hammer and suddenly there were two living goats again. One of them was lame, which made Thor angry enough to threaten to slaughter the entire family, even though they had given him hospitality for the night. In order to spare all of their lives, the peasants offered Thor Thialfi, the culprit, and his sister Roskva as slaves for eternity. Thor accepted at once.

The thunder god had various other adventures with giants, often involving Loki. The recovery of his hammer from Thrym involved him disguising himself as Freya. He destroyed Geirrod and his daughters as well as the previously amicable giant Hymir, the owner of an extremely large cauldron.

THE QUEST FOR HYMIR'S CAULDRON

Thor and Tyr entered Hymir's hall in search of this vessel and were entertained hospitably by him. The following day, however, Thor behaved very badly. He and Hymir decided to go fishing together; when the giant suggested that Thor should find some bait, the god slew Hymir's biggest bull, Himinbrioter, in order to put its head on his hook. Thor then rowed their boat far out to sea and caught the World Serpent, Jormungand; he was just about to despatch the beast when Hymir, terrified, cut the line. Thor hit the giant with his hammer, knocking him overboard, but Hymir swam to shore and met Thor there amicably. The two then breakfasted on a couple of whales Hymir had caught; after the repast the giant challenged the god to smash his beaker. Thor threw the vessel at everything in sight but without success; finally he shattered it by throwing it at Hymir's forehead.

Hymir then told Thor and Tyr that they could have the cauldron; Tyr could not lift it and even Thor could do so only with difficulty.

Above: A tenth- or eleventh-century silver Swedish pendant representing Thor's hammer, found in a Viking grave at Öland.

Right: The giant Hymir (on the right) out on a fishing expedition with the god Thor, who is attempting to catch Jormungand, the World Serpent. A fragment from the tenth-century cross found at Gosforth, Cumbria.

Opposite: An eighth-century Swedish bronze matrix used for making helmet decorations. The boar's head indicates that these warriors were dedicated to the cult of Frey, whose boar was called Hildisvin.

As the gods were leaving Hymir summoned his fellow frost giants who attacked the gods, but Thor killed them all with his hammer. The two gods then triumphantly returned with the cauldron to the hall of Aegir.

In fact, it is curious that any of the giant race should show anything other than loathing for this god, so many of them did he slay, yet there are some examples of them helping him – for example, his life would have been forfeited had it not been for the prior assistance of a giantess called Grid. She gave a night's lodging to Thor and Loki as they travelled towards the hall of the giant Geirrod. After Loki had fallen asleep, Grid told a drunken Thor that Geirrod was planning to kill him and that he was foolish to make the journey without his hammer and girdle of strength. She gave

Right: A bronze statuette of Frey from Lunda, Sweden. The god of fruit and crops and the sun and rain, his primary role as fertility god is extremely obvious.

him gloves made of iron, a replacement girdle of strength, along with an unbreakable staff with which to combat Geirrod.

FREY

Frey was one of the Vanir who came to Asgard as a hostage at the end of the struggle between the Vanir and the Aesir; he was the son of Njord and the twin brother of Freya, whom at one point he also married. His name is often given as Freyr. He was a fertility god and god of summer, and the cult associated with him seems to have been pretty unpleasant, involving such practices as human sacrifice. It was also the custom to carry around a carved image of the god on a cart, accompanied by a priestess, so that the faithful could make offerings and sacrifices to it and therefore ensure good harvests and fertile marriages.

He was connected with the image of the boar Gullinbursti; this creature had shining bristles that lit up the world as it flew through the air. Frey also owned the ship Skidbladnir, which could fly through the sky and, although large enough to carry all the gods, their horses and equipment, could, when not in use, be folded up and put in a pocket. Another useful possession was his sword, which under its own motivation would start slaying his enemies as soon as it was drawn from its sheath. His horse was called Blodughofi. His hall was in Alfheim, the realm of light elves.

THE WOOING OF GERDA

Frey is regarded as one of the three major Norse gods – the other two being Odin and Thor – yet there are surprisingly few tales about him. The most important concerns his love for a frost giantess, Gerda, the daughter of Gymir and Angrboda. Frey first caught sight of her when he was trespassing on Hlidskialf, Odin's

great throne from where everything in the nine worlds was visible. Gerda was a figure of pulsating light (she is often associated with the Aurora Borealis, or Northern Lights) and Frey was instantly stricken with lust for her. He pined for ages afterwards until Njord summoned his best servant, Skirnir, and told him to find out what the matter was. Skirnir quizzed Frey and eventually got the truth out of him. The god realised that the union he sought with Gerda would be unconscionable to gods and mortals alike, yet still he craved her. So he asked Skirnir to go to Gerda and attempt to woo her; the servant agreed on condition that Frey lend him his sword and horse. He also took with him eleven of the golden apples of

Above left: The skull of a woman sacrificed at a Viking ship burial at Ballyteare, Isle of Man, in the ninth century. The top of her head was choped off.

Above: A twelfth-century tapestry from Skog Church, Halsingland, Sweden. The three figures on the left are believed to represent Odin, Thor and Frey.

eternal youth as well as Odin's magic ring, Draupnir.

Blodughofi bore Skirnir swiftly to Jotunheim, where he found that Gymir's hall was surrounded by curtains of coruscating flame; the servant spurred the horse to greater speed and they shot through the fire. They found that the hall was guarded by huge, horrific hounds, who set up such a howling that Gerda was alerted to their arrival. She realised that the visitor had been sent by Frey, who had slain her brother Beli in a brawl, but asked him in for a bowl of mead. He immediately began to urge Frey's suit, to which she responded forthrightly. Skirnir then tried to bribe her with the apples and with Draupnir, to which she replied in both cases with equally negative frankness.

THE WINNING OF GERDA

Skirnir then told her that he would chop her head off if she did not agree to obey Frey's summons, but she told him that she was not afraid of him. The servant finally used his deadliest threat. Carved on his staff were runes, and he used the magical power of these to lay on her a curse so vile that she was terrified into acquiescence. Refuse and, forever afterwards, he told her, she would be devoured by

lust yet remain celibate; be consumed with hunger yet find that all food tasted brackish to her; be confined by Hel's gates and forced to watch that miserable prospect, knowing that she was becoming a repulsive hag. The only way to avoid this fate was to accede to Frey's demands. This she agreed to do, but said that she would not meet the god for nine nights. Finally the two married. Despite the shocking way in which she had been treated, she came to love him, bearing his child Fiolnir.

LOKI

Loki, the wizard of lies, the god of mischief and deception, is the most fascinating of all the members of the Norse pantheon, not just because of his wiles and cunning but because he shows that rarest of things in a mythological personage: character development. Although he was never to be trusted, in the early days he helped Odin create the world and was then useful to the other gods on countless occasions. Later his mischief took on a more malevolent nature, as when he chopped off the hair of Sif. But then he became actively evil, arranging for the murder of Balder and committing other hideous crimes.

Loki married three times. His first wife was called Glut and she bore him the children

Einmyria and Eisa; all three names refer to fire and its warmth, since in one of his aspects Loki was the charming god of the fireside, relaxation and leisure. For this reason the peasant classes maintained that he was the greatest of all the gods. The offspring of his second marriage were less pleasant. This time his wife was a giantess called Angrboda and their children were Hel, the goddess of death; Jormungand, the World Serpent; and Fenris, the monstrous wolf who came to threaten the very existence of the gods. Loki's third wife was the beautiful Sigyn; their two children were Narvi and Vali (not to be confused with the god called Vali).

LOKI'S CAPRICIOUSNESS

There are far more tales about Loki than about any of the other gods, including stories illustrating his helpfulness, as when the giantess Skadi came to Asgard seeking vengeance for the slaying of her father, Thiassi. Loki entertained her with lewd knockabout humour until she relented and became the wife of Njord.

But Loki could be randomly cruel. One day he, Odin and Hoenir were out walking when Loki spotted an otter by a riverbank preparing to eat a salmon. The god threw a stone accurately and killed the animal. However, this was no ordinary otter but Otter, one of the sons of the dwarfish king Hreidmar. So began the whole miserable business of Andvari's gold and the devastation of the family of Hreidmar.

As we saw, Loki's children by the giantess Angrboda were Hel, Jormungand and Fenris. The marriage had been unauthorised and so

Right: A fragment from a tenth-century cross found at Michael, Isle of Man, showing Frey and Gerda. She is the bird-headed figure and he the tethered stallion.

Right: Part of a Viking cross slab at Maughold, Isle of Man, showing Loki crouching with the stone with which he is about to kill Otter (depicted with a salmon in his mouth).

he tried to keep the children hidden in a cave, but they grew rapidly and Odin discovered their existence. He determined to get rid of them before they grew so large that they threatened the world. He cast Hel into Niflheim, in which dismal realm she reigned gloomily as the goddess of death. The snake Jormungand he threw into the sea, where it grew so huge that it soon encircled the entire world and was able to swallow its own tail.

THE BINDING OF FENRIS

Fenris, however, he brought to Asgard to try to educate the wolf into the ways of gentleness. There Fenris continued to grow in both size and ferocity and the gods decided to bind him so securely that he would never be able to threaten them again. After Fenris had broken two chains the dwarfs gave the gods the slender strand Gleipnir. Fenris agreed to be tied up in it only if one of the gods would put a hand in Fenris' mouth as a guarantee that no magic was involved; Tyr thus lost his hand. The wolf was then placed beneath the ground, where he howled with great abandon. To silence him the Aesir put a sword vertically in his mouth, with its point in his palate; blood flowed forth to form a great river.

THE SHEARING OF SIF

Loki's tricks became more and more spiteful. With his lies and his habit of revealing secrets he constantly stirred the gods against each other. One of his worst tricks was shearing

Right: The western face of Gosforth Cross, Cumbria. At the bottom is the chained Loki.

Far right: The southern face of Gosforth Cross. At the bottom is the bound Fenris; above is Odin on horseback.

Sif's magnificent hair. It was as a result of this and his wager with Brock and Sindri that Loki suffered the agony of having his lips stitched up.

LOKI'S TORMENT

The gods' merriment over his torment was probably what turned his petty maliciousness into a vindictive lust to destroy them. He started with Balder, and later turned up uninvited at a banquet to insult all the gods in the most vitriolic terms, as recorded in a riveting *flyting* ('insult poem'). The gods decided that enough was enough and decided to bind him.

Finally having caught the shape-shifter who had assumed the form of a fish, Odin, Thor and Kvasir took him to a deep cavern, induced Loki's son Vali to become a wolf and rip out the throat of his other son, Narvi. From Narvi's corpse they extracted the entrails and these they used to tie up Loki to three great rocks, later turning the guts into iron. The giantess Skadi hung a serpent over Loki's head so that its venom would drip into his face for the rest of eternity. Every drop of venom caused him unspeakable pain.

At the great battle of Ragnarok, the gods were to regret their cruelty to Loki.

Below: A detail from a c. *twelfth-century wooden portal at Hylestad Church, Setesdal, Norway, showing the dragon Fafnir being slain by Sigurd.*

VIKING
GODDESSES

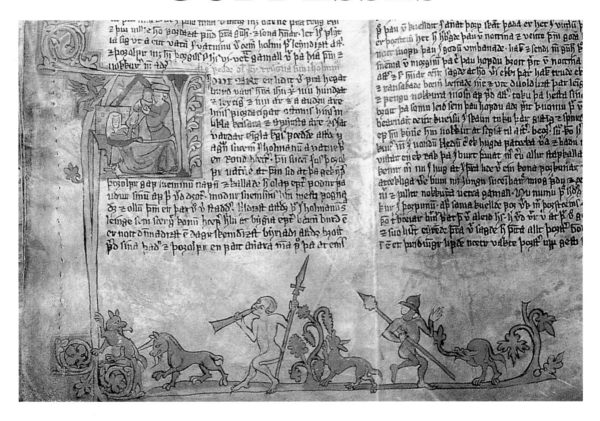

Preceding page: A detail from an Icelandic manuscript copy of the Flateyjarbok, *part of the Poetic Edda.*

Right: Frigga pictured with some of her handmaidens, who were goddesses in their own right.

The stories of four of the most important Viking goddesses are told here: Frigga, the favourite wife of Odin, mother of Balder and the pre-eminent Viking goddess; Freya, who, although she was no great paragon of virtue, was one of the most important and respected members of the Norse pantheon; Idun, the apple-carrying guardian of the gods' eternal youth; and the golden-haired Sif, whose tresses were compared to abundant stalks of corn.

FRIGGA

Second wife of Odin and mother of Balder, Frigga was the most important goddess in the Norse pantheon. Because of her connection with fertility there was obviously a marked overlap between her responsibilities and those of Frey and Freya. It seems likely that all three had initially had the same identity before Frigga

was separated from Frey/Freya and then these two likewise became divided from each other. However, in some branches of Teutonic myth Frigga and Freya are regarded as identical – both, for example, have falcon skins that they can wear to fly around the nine worlds.

A FERTILITY GODDESS

However, Frigga seems always to have been a much gentler fertility goddess than Freya: where the latter represented rampant sex and was associated with a good deal of violence, Frigga was much more associated with that aspect of fertility related to placid domesticity, conjugal happiness and maternity. It should not be assumed, however, that she was a consistently obedient spouse: the myths suggest that early on she enjoyed adultery with Odin's brothers Ve and Vili and later, often enough, she would work to trick Odin in order to advance the cause of someone she preferred. Frigga and Odin often walked around Midgard together. A major legend of one of these ventures concerns Agnar and Geirrod; here Frigga successfully tricked her husband. Another tale of her wiles concerns a war between the

Above: A beautifully worked bronze and gilt brooch found in a Viking grave in Norway.

35

Right: A gilt brooch found in a Viking grave in Sweden. It dates from between the ninth and eleventh centuries AD.

Below: A dress fastener dating from the Viking period. It is made of bronze and gilt.

Vandals and Winilers. Frigga's hall was called Fensalir, and she spent much of her time sitting there spinning golden thread or brightly coloured clouds.

ODIN'S CONSORT

Her parentage is something of a conundrum. According to some versions she was the daughter of Odin and the very early goddess Jörd; alternatively she was Jörd's sister, both of them being daughters of the giantess Fiorgyn. Either way, she became Odin's wife and, alone among all the other deities, was permitted to sit upon Hlidskialf, his great throne from which one could see everything that was going on in all the worlds. In addition to this shared omniscience she also had the ability to foretell the future, but she was loath to tell others what she saw there.

She was, perhaps, a little too fond of glorious attire for her own good, but that seems to have been her only notable sin. It was a sin that could get her into trouble, though. Odin had erected a statue of himself and had placed a piece of gold inside it. Frigga was keen to have a magnificent necklace made for her by the dwarfs, and so she stole the gold for the dwarfs to use. Odin was less than amused when he later found that it had been made from gold stolen from his statue. He summoned the dwarfs and demanded that they tell him the name of the thief, but they refused. Odin next composed runes to give the statue the power of speech. Frigga was terrified to hear of all this and summoned her attendant Fulla to help her avoid discovery. Fulla returned in the company of a revoltingly ugly dwarf, who promised that he would stop the statue speaking if Frigga slept with him. No sooner said than done, and the following morning the dwarf magically made the guards fall into a deep sleep and shattered the statue. Odin was furious and left Asgard for seven months. During this time, Ve and Vili took power – and also, according to some sources, enjoyed Frigga's sexual favours.

AN EARTH MOTHER

Frigga is identified with many other goddesses in various mythologies. A complete list would be impossible: here we can note Bertha, Brechta, Eastre (from which the term 'Easter' comes), Gode, Hlodin, Holda, Horn, Nerthus, Ostara and Wode. As the archetypal earth mother, of course, she has parallels in almost all of the world's mythologies.

FREYA

To call Freya a fertility goddess is to euphemise: she was, quite simply, the goddess of sex. Daughter of Njord and twin sister of Frey, she was one of the three Vanir who came to Asgard as hostages at the end of

Right: Arthur Rackham's vision of the beautiful sex goddess Freya, with her cats purring at her feet.

Above: Details of the stern of the Oseberg longship, which is intricately carved with symbols drawn from Viking mythology and sacred belief.

the war between the Vanir and the Aesir; there is some confusion between her and Frigga.

The Aesir were so enchanted by her beauty that they granted to her the realm of Folkvang and the hall Sessrymnir; this latter was so well built that it was regarded as impregnable unless the doors were opened by Freya herself. Her chariot was pulled either by her boar Hildisvini, or by a number of cats. She owned a falcon coat which she could use to fly around the world in the guise of that bird. Horses were involved in her cult, for reasons, it appears, of orgiastic sex. Besides her role in terms of sex and beauty she had a somewhat grimmer aspect, because she often led parties of Valkyries down to fetch the dead from battlefields, bringing them back to her hall so that they could enjoy all the benefits of the afterlife under her patronage.

A PROMISCUOUS GODDESS

Her first husband was called Od (or Odur), but he deserted her, and thereafter she wept golden tears of grief at all opportunities – such as there were, for her life thereafter was one of unbridled promiscuity. Counting her various conquests is a fraught matter, but we can list her brother Frey (it is possible that the two of them were originally a single god, and that the tale of their sexual relations represents an explanation of the way that, by the time the Eddas were being written, they had become two), Odin and other gods, a man called Ottar, not to mention four very important dwarfs. She did have her standards though: she refused to sleep with the giant Hrungnir and likewise with the giant Thrym, even though in the case of the latter she was fervently encouraged to do so by Loki and Thor.

In the story of her exploits with the four

Left: A Swedish bronze matrics, dating from about the eighth century, used for fashioning plaques for Viking helmets. It depicts a man with a boar on each side.

Right: Part of a belt buckle found in a sixth-century chief's grave at Aker, Norway. The work was done in silver and gilt, together with niello, gold and garnets.

dwarfs, she was exploring the world one night when she came across the smithy of four dwarfs called the Brisings, or Brosings. They were in the process of making an ornament (the Brisingamen, generally assumed to have been a necklace) of such exquisite beauty that Freya could hardly believe her eyes. There was nothing that the goddess would not do to possess that treasure: when the dwarfs declared that she could have it only if she spent a night of lust with each of them in turn she therefore readily assented.

LOKI STEALS THE BRISINGAMEN

What she had not realised was that Loki had seen her leaving Asgard and had followed her. The wizard of lies rushed to tell Odin of her prostitution, and the leader of the Aesir was furious – he longed for Freya himself, so to discover that she was disporting herself with four dwarfs hurt him grievously. He told Loki that he was to steal the Brisingamen from Freya, otherwise there would be terrible punishments in store. Loki pointed out that her hall Sessrymnir could only be entered with Freya's permission, but Odin's response was to become even more threatening, so Loki thus

Left: Detail of an eighth-century stela found in Gotland, Sweden, showing a Scandinavian warrior on horseback.

decided that he would do his best.

Loki had the advantage that he could change his shape at will. It took him a long time before he discovered a tiny aperture though which he could squirm his way into Sessrymnir, but in the end he managed it. There he saw the lovely form of Freya sprawled on her bed but, alas, in such a position that he was unable to reach the clasp of the Brisingamen. Turning himself into a flea, he bit Freya so that she turned over in her sleep, exposing the clasp. Loki swiftly returned to his own form and let himself out of Sessrymnir, taking the Brisingamen with him.

What happened next is a matter of debate. According to some versions, the god Heimdall – who could hear even grass growing – heard Loki as he was perpetrating the theft and pursued him. The two waged a battle involving considerable shape-shifting until Loki was finally persuaded that he should return the

Brisingamen to Freya. An alternative is that Loki took the necklace to Odin. When, next morning, Freya discovered the loss of her precious treasure she realised that the only possible culprit had to be Loki and went to Odin to complain. Odin instead announced that, as punishment, she should in future adopt as part of her responsibilities the spreading of

warfare and misery, otherwise he would keep the Brisingamen forever. Freya agreed to the bargain: she needed the necklace almost more than life itself.

IDUN

Idun, the wife of Bragi, was the goddess of spring and the guardian of the gods' eternal

Below: Pieces of a Viking chess set made from walrus ivory between 1135 and 1150 and found on the Isle of Lewis, Scotland.

youth. This youthfulness was incorporated in the form of golden apples, which she kept in a magic basket; no matter how many apples she removed from the basket to give to the gods during their feasting there was always still the same number left. Idun reserved her apples exclusively for the gods, who thereafter remained young and vigorous while all other beings grew old and died. Naturally the apples were coveted by the dwarfs and giants and this fact led to Idun's major adventure.

THE GODS GO HUNGRY

Odin, Hoenir and Loki were one day wandering in the world when they became hungry. Spotting a nearby herd of cattle they killed one of the beasts, made a fire and roasted it. However, when they kicked away the embers of the fire and sat down to eat they discovered that the ox was hardly cooked at all. They tried again, but still without success. Then a huge eagle spoke to them, saying that its magic had stopped the flames from cooking the flesh and offering the three Aesir a deal: the eagle would remove the spell but they were to give the bird as much to eat as it wanted.

LOKI STRIKES A DEAL

The bargain was struck but the Aesir had not reckoned on the eagle's appetite, leaving the gods with not much to eat. This drove Loki into a fury and he picked up a branch and plunged it into the bird's neck. The eagle dropped the meat and flew off, still impaled by the branch which Loki now found his hands were stuck to. They flew low over the ground so that Loki was bumped and bruised until he

Right: An illustration from F L Spence's Rhine Legends *(1915) depicting Odin and Brunhild. The Vikings admired golden hair.*

was in agony. He screamed for mercy and finally the bird agreed that it would release him
if he would promise to do something for it:
lead Idun out from the safety of Asgard so
that she could be captured. Loki agreed and
the eagle – in fact a giant called Thiassi in
disguise – let him go.

IDUN IS ABDUCTED

Loki went to Idun and told her that he had
discovered a grove where apples exactly like
her magic ones grew. Credulously she accepted
his offer to lead her to this place. However,
as soon as they were out of Asgard, he deserted her. Thiassi, again in his guise as an
eagle, swooped down from the skies and car-
ried the goddess away to his hall, crowing that
at last he had captured the gift of eternal youth.
He was deeply chagrined to discover that Idun
refused to let him have a single apple.

THE AESIR BEGIN TO AGE

It was not long before things at Asgard began
to go badly wrong. The Aesir, who had assumed that Idun had gone away with her min-
strel husband Bragi on one of his ramblings,
became worried about her, especially when
they started wrinkling with age and losing their
reason to senility. Odin summoned the Aesir
to a conference, and when they were gathered
they discovered that all were present except
Loki. It became plain that Loki was connected with Idun's disappearance and the other
gods made it clear to him that he had to bring
Idun back. He therefore borrowed Freya's falcon skin and flew off to Thiassi's hall,
Thrymheim. Since the giant was absent, Loki

*Right: Detail from a wooden portal in
Norway's Hylestad Church, depicting the
dwarf Regin reforging Sigurd's sword.*

44

Left: A silver figure of a Valkyrie holding up a drinking horn found in an eleventh-century Viking grave.

turned Idun into a nut and, clutching her in his claws, flew back towards Asgard.

THIASSI IS THWARTED

When Thiassi found the goddess gone he was furious. He adopted the form of a huge eagle once more and set off in hot pursuit of Loki. And when the gods looked out from Asgard to watch for Loki's return they saw not only the falcon but also, in chase, the great black eagle. The Aesir swiftly gathered up a large heap of fuel and, as the falcon flopped exhaustedly into Asgard bearing its precious burden, they set light to the fuel so that Thiassi flew straight into a wall of flames. Burnt and stunned, the eagle crumpled to the ground and was swiftly despatched by the Aesir.

Another legend about Idun has largely been lost to us. It seems that one day she accidentally fell into Niflheim, where she went into a frozen and horrified coma. Odin sent Bragi and a couple of the other gods down there after her with some skins to warm her, but they were unable to get her to respond. In the end Bragi told the other two to leave them there, and that he would keep his wife company until she was ready to go. What happened next is, sadly, unrecorded.

SIF

Not a lot is known about the goddess Sif. She seems to have been a fertility goddess whose prominence had faded by the time the chroniclers were writing their tales. Thor was her

Right: An exquisitely decorated golden Norwegian plate, dating from the fifth century.

Left: The chained Loki is tended by his faithful wife Sigyn, who catches the serpent's dripping venom in a bowl.

second husband; to her first, an anonymous frost giant, she bore a son called Uller. Her sons by Thor were called Magni and Modi.

SIF'S UNWANTED HAIR LOSS

The reason for guessing that she was connected with fertility is that she had a mane of beautiful golden hair that reached all the way to the ground; this is taken to represent abundant corn. She was extremely proud of her hair, as was Thor, so neither of them were pleased when one night as she slept someone came along and cut it all off. When such things happened in Asgard the culprit was invariably Loki. Thor responded to the situation with his usual subtlety and so a few moments later a battered Loki discovered that he had promised to get Sif a new head of hair.

Such things are not easy to procure and Loki knew that he had no alternative but to seek the aid of the mastercraftsmen of the nine worlds, the dwarfs of Svartalfaheim. He went to the smithy of a dwarf called Dvalin and persuaded him to make the hair. The dwarf did a miraculous job and, despite the fact that all Loki offered by way of payment was a string of empty promises, went on to create Frey's magic ship Skidbladnir, as well as Odin's magic spear Gungnir.

LOKI CHALLENGES THE DWARFS

Loki was amazed by the magnificence of these gifts and also by the gullibility of the dwarf. On his way back to Asgard it struck him that other dwarfs could be similarly duped. Instants later he was showing the three treasures to two dwarfs called Brock and Sindri (or Eitri) and enthusing to them over how, surely, no

dwarf could ever hope again to make anything as fine. In fact, he bet the two dwarfs that if they could craft anything better, as judged by the gathered Aesir, they could chop off his head. The dwarfs agreed.

GULLINBURSTI AND DRAUPNIR

Sindri told Brock to keep the bellows blowing consistently while he went off to mutter the appropriate runes. As Brock worked an insect stung his hand, but he did not miss a beat. When Sindri reappeared they pulled from the forge Gullinbursti, the great magical boar that Frey would use to ride across the sky. Then they set to work making the next artefact, and Brock was again ineffectually stung. This time the product of the forge was the magical golden ring (or armlet) Draupnir, which, every ninth night, would produce eight others identical to it; in time it was to become the property of Odin. Loki realised that these treasures were beyond compare.

THE CREATION OF MIÖLNIR

This time, as Brock was pumping away, the gadfly stung him on the eyelid so that blood ran into the dwarf's eye. Blinded, he took his hand from the bellows for a moment to wipe the blood away. The object the two dwarfs drew from the forge was the mighty hammer Miölnir, which would become the property of Thor. It was perfect in every respect except that its handle was perhaps a trifle too short.

THE JUDGEMENT OF THE GODS

Loki and the dwarfs went to Asgard with all six of these wonderful gifts, which were handed to their various recipients and the Aesir marvelled at all of them. The god was not particularly worried because of the imperfection of Miölnir. Sif's golden hair, everyone agreed, was if anything more splendid than her previous mane had been. However, they pointed out that Miölnir was the most valuable of all the gifts because it could guard them from the predations of the giants. The gods laughed as Loki tried to bargain his way out of this one before finally fleeing the hall. Brock begged Thor to bring the wizard of lies back so that the wager could be completed and the huge god fetched Loki and placed him in front of the others; all waited for the execution.

Left: A detail from a copy of the Cannin Casket (dated about AD 1000), now in the National Museum, Copenhagen, Denmark.

However, Loki had been thinking further and realised that although this head was forfeit to Brock and Sindri, his neck was not. The dwarfs had to find some way of decapitating him without harming his neck. The Aesir and dwarfs realised that Loki had a point, but the reason that the dwarfs had wanted Loki's head was to stop his mischievous lying. Brock therefore said that he would be content to sew up Loki's lips, and this he did with Sindri's magic awl. The god's agony was excruciating and he ran from the place screaming as he tore away the thongs. The Aesir laughed all the more merrily at his discomfiture, which was perhaps unwise of them, because thereafter Loki became ever more malicious.

Below: A detail from an intricately crafted tenth-century Danish neck yoke for a pair of horses.

A GLOSSARY OF GODS AND GODDESSES

Right: Aegir, the god of the sea, depicted with his wife Ran, who used her net to snatch sailors from the decks of their ships.

Preceding page: A piece of modern sculpture at Bratahild shows representations of Viking symbols.

Norse mythology is very complex, so as a reference aid for the reader here is a list of the major Viking gods and goddesses, listed in alphabetical order.

AEGIR (HLER): the god of the sea.

BALDER: a beautiful and gentle god, slain inadvertently by his brother Hoder as a result of Loki's trickery.

BOLWERK: one of the pseudonyms used by Odin for his adventures among mortals.

BRAGI: the god of music, poetry and eloquence, the son of Odin and Gunnlod, the giantess whom he had seduced. Bragi married Idun. Odin carved runes on his tongue and gave him the job of composing songs to honour the gods and the dead heroes in Valhalla.

DELLINGER (DELLING): the god of dawn and the third husband of Night, or Nott. Their son was Dag.

EIRA (EYRA): one of the attendants of Frigga and also the goddess of medicine.

FJORGYN (ERDA, JÖRD): the Earth goddess and one of Odin's three wives. She and Odin combined to produce Thor.

FORSETI: the god of justice and truth, son of Balder and Nanna. Forseti had the ability to talk so eloquently that foes would make peace; if they didn't, Forseti would then strike them dead.

FREY (FREYR, FRO): one of the Vanir race of gods. The son of Njord, Frey came to Asgard as a hostage along with his father and sister Freya. Frey was a fertility god.

FREYA (FREYJA): the goddess of sex and later also of war and death. One of the Vanir, she came to Asgard as a hostage accompanied by her father Njord and brother Frey. She married the god Od, who deserted her; thereafter she divided her time between mourning his absence and being promiscuous. In the German version of the Teutonic myth she is identified with Frigga.

FRIDLEEF: one of the pseudonyms used by Frey for his adventures among mortals.

FRIGGA (BERTHA, FRIGG, HOLDA, NERTHUS, WODE): the most important goddess of Asgard; one of the three wives of Odin and the mother of Balder and Hoder. She was the principal goddess of fertility. Ve and Vili are reputed to have slept with her, as is Ull. There has been a certain amount of confusion between her and Freya, to the extent that in the German version of the Teutonic myth they were regarded as the same deity.

FULLA: a goddess who acted as Frigga's attendant and messenger; she was herself a fertility goddess.

GANGRAD: one of the pseudonyms used by Odin for his adventures among mortals.

GEFJON (GEFION): a goddess who served as one of Frigga's attendants. She slept with Gylfi, king of Sweden, and was consequently allowed to claim as much of his nation as she could plough within a 24-hour period. She fetched four huge oxen, who were the four

Left: Hermod bids farewell to Balder and Nanna, believing that the world would fulfil Hel's condition for releasing the god.

sons she had borne to a giant, and within the requisite time wrenched free a colossal area of Sweden, which her sons towed out to sea. The tract of land is now the island known as Zealand; the hole in Sweden was soon filled up with water, becoming Lake Malaren.

GERSEMI: one of Freya's and Od's two daughters (Hnoss was the other).

GNA (LIOD): a servant of Frigga who acted as the great goddess' messenger. Perhaps her most significant mission was to bring the apple of fertility to the mortal Rerir.

GRIMNIR: one of the pseudonyms used by Odin for his adventures among mortals.

HEIMDALL: a somewhat puzzling god born from nine giantess mothers (the Wave Maidens) simultaneously. As Riger he wandered around Midgard impregnating women to found the serf, peasant and warrior races. He was the guardian of the rainbow bridge to Asgard, Bifrost.

HEL: a goddess or a monster, a daughter of Loki and Angrboda, who ruled over Niflheim. Opinions differed over whether she was alive or dead. After the death of the god Balder she was asked by Hermod if she would simply allow the much-loved god to leave her premises; her response was that she didn't think that Balder was nearly as much loved as all that. She was similarly unsympathetic when Bragi turned up hoping to recover Idun. Ull, in his role as god of winter, was supposed to spend

a couple of months each year as Hel's lover. Some versions of the mythology say that one of the Norns, Skuld, was the same person as Hel. She and her ghostly army will support the other gods at Ragnarok, after which her domain will be consumed by flames.

HERMOD (IRMIN): the son of Odin and Frigga. He welcomed the heroes to Valhalla and otherwise acted as the equivalent of the Greek god Hermes. His most spectacular errand was to Hel in an effort to recover the god Balder from the realm of the dead.

HLER: according to a version of the creation myth, one of the first gods.

HLIN: a goddess who attended Frigga. The goddess of consolation, she was extremely beautiful; she kissed away mourners' tears, relieved grief and heard the prayers of mortals, passing them on to the supreme goddess Frigga with compassionate recommendations that she answer them positively.

Left: An eighteenth-century illustration of Hermod riding down to Hel on Sleipnir in his attempt to rescue Balder.

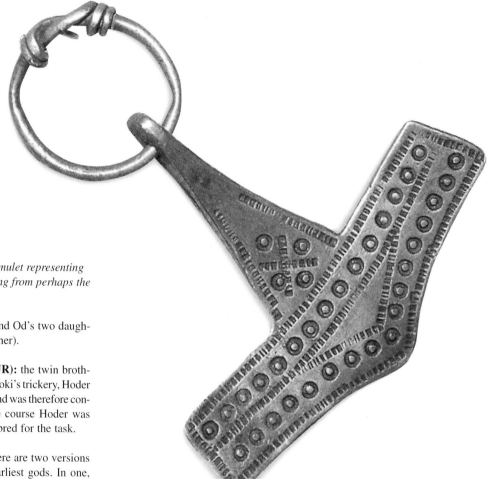

Right: A silver Danish amulet representing Thor's hammer and dating from perhaps the tenth century.

HNOSS: one of Freya and Od's two daughters (Gersemi was the other).

HODER (HOD, HODUR): the twin brother of Balder. Because of Loki's trickery, Hoder unwittingly slew Balder and was therefore condemned to death. In due course Hoder was killed by Vali, specially bred for the task.

HOENIR (HONIR): there are two versions of the story about the earliest gods. In one, Odin and his brothers Ve and Vili gave the human species the gifts that it has. The alternative is that Odin's first brothers were Hoenir and Loki. According to this version Hoenir gave to humanity the dual gifts of motion and the senses.

IDUN: the goddess of spring and of immortal youth. She was the daughter of the dwarf Ivald and the wife of the god Bragi.

KARI: according to some versions of the creation myth, the sons of the giant Ymir were Hler (the sea), Kari (the air) and Loki or Lodur (fire). These three gods gave birth to the giants or monsters Beli, Fenris, Grendel, Gymir, Hel, Mimir, Thiassi and Thrym.

KVASIR: a somewhat enigmatic figure, in that it is uncertain whether he was a god or merely a supernatural being. If a god, he was probably one of the Vanir but with an admixture of Aesir. He was brought into existence at the end of the war between the Aesir and the Vanir; as a token of the truce all the gods spat into a ceremonial vase and from their spittle they generated Kvasir. He became renowned for his wisdom and virtue and was consequently murdered in his sleep by two dwarfs called Fialar and Galar, who wished to take his wisdom for the benefit of the dwarf race. They drained his blood into three containers (a kettle or cauldron called Odhroerir and two bowls called Boden and Son), mixed it with honey and fermented it to produce a brew that turned the drinker into a poet.

LODUR: according to one version of the creation myth, Odin's brothers were Hoenir and Lodur; these three gave humanity its life. Lodur's contributions were blood and a healthy complexion. Lodur can be equated with Loki.

LOFN: an attendant of Frigga. A beautiful maiden, Lofn had the responsibility for easing the path of true love.

LOKI: the 'wizard of lies' and in many ways the most interesting of all the gods of Asgard. Loki was related to Odin, but the nature of the relationship was muddled. He came to Asgard either as of right or because Odin entered into a blood-brotherhood with him.

MAGNI: a son of Thor and the giantess Iarnsaxa. He rescued his father after the latter's duel with the giant Hrungnir. After Ragnarok Magni and his brother Modi will possess Thor's hammer Miölnir.

MIMIR: the wisest god of all the Aesir; he – or, at least, his head – guarded a spring (Mimir's Well) at the base of Yggdrasil. There is some confusion regarding his decapitation, but it seems that he and Hoenir were sent by the Aesir to the Vanir as hostages to protect the truce agreed between the two families of gods. The Vanir did not like Hoenir so they killed Mimir. It is possible that he was the creator of the sword Miming. Odin made a habit of consulting Mimir's head on occasions when he needed advice. In some versions it is reported that Odin's loss of one eye came about because he had to give it to Mimir's head as a down payment for this counselling service.

Left: Part of a Viking sword, strongly influenced by the English style, with a silver and gold hilt found at Dybäck, Skane.

MODI: a son of Thor and the giantess Iarnsaxa. After Ragnarok he and his brother Magni will possess Thor's hammer Miölnir.

NANNA: the wife of Balder.

NERTHUS (HLODIN): the wife of Njord; a goddess often equated with Frigga.

NJORD: the father of Frey and Freya; one of the Vanir; a god of the sea who slowly attained ascendance over the Aesir sea god Aegir. He was the husband of both the giantess Skadi and the goddess Nerthus.

NORNS: the three goddesses concerned with destiny. Called Skuld ('being'), Urd ('fate') and Verdandi ('necessity'), they were obviously closely related in concept to the Fates of Greek mythology. They sprinkled Yggdrasil with holy water every day so that it would stay in tiptop condition. They were also keen weavers, producing webs of great vastness but haphazard design, as if they did not know what the outcome of their weaving was likely to be. Two of the sisters, Urd (who was incredibly old) and Verdandi (who was young and lovely) were generally pretty friendly toward mortals, but Skuld was swift to take offence over the most trivial slight or perceived slight.

Skuld also had a destructive habit of ripping up the webs made by the three sisters when they were nearly finished.

NOTT: the goddess of night; daughter of the giant Norvi. She had three lovers/husbands: Naglfari, to whom she bore Aud; Annar, who gave her the daughter Erda; and Dellinger, whose son by her was called Dag.

OD (ODUR): the first husband of Freya. She loved him madly but he had a roving heart and departed in search of mortal women. Freya spent the rest of eternity in a confusing mix of mourning and copulation.

ODIN (WODAN, WODEN, WOTAN): the son of Börr and Bestla and the father of Thor, Balder, Hoder, Tyr, Bragi, Heimdall, Ull, Vidar, Hermod and Vali. His wives were Fjorgyn, Frigga and Rind. He was the chief god in the Norse pantheon. One of his habits was to roam around Midgard in human guise seducing and impregnating women; many mortals were therefore able to trace their ancestry back to the chief Aesir, Odin.

RAN: the wife of Aegir and like him associated with the sea. She had a net which she used to drag down drowning people.

Opposite: Njord and Skadi are depicted on their way from Asgard to Noatûn after their honeymoon.

Right: Part of the Cumbrian Gosforth Cross, showing Odin being attacked by a winged dragon during Ragnarok.

Right: An illustration of the giantess Gunnlod in the process of being seduced by Odin, who wanted her mead of poetry.

Far right: Odin being tormented between two fires at the palace of King Geirrod.

Right: Torshavn ('Thor's Harbour') in the Faeroe Islands. Thor is still a popular name in the Faeroes and Iceland.

Below: Bronze metalwork from a Swedish Viking grave, apparently showing Thor fishing for Jormungand, the World Serpent.

RIGER: one of the pseudonyms used by Heimdall for his adventures among mortals.

RIND (RINDA): a goddess mentioned only as the third wife of Odin, who gave birth to his son Vali. She was by all accounts frigid, being the goddess of the frozen soil. There is some confusion between her and the mortal Rind, daughter of King Billing; it is possible that the goddess and woman were originally the same character.

SAGA: a mistress of Odin whom the god visited for a daily drink at her hall, Sokvabek.

SAETERE: the Teutonic god of agriculture, possibly one of the many personae of Loki.
SIF: the goddess who married Thor and bore his stepson (by Odin), Ull. She was exceptionally proud of her golden hair, so Loki cut it all off while she slept.

SIGYN: the third wife of Loki and the one who was unremittingly faithful to him; she bore his mortal sons Narve and Vali. Even after Loki had been thrown out of Asgard because of his crimes Sigyn remained loyal to him.

SKULD: one of the Norns.

SNOTRA: one of Frigga's attendants and also the omniscient goddess of virtue.

SUMMER: one of the early gods. He was loved by all except Winter.

SVASUD: a beautiful and gentle god whose son was Summer.

SYN: a goddess who guarded the door of Frigga's palace against unwelcome visitors. Once she had decided to refuse someone entry there was no possibility of changing her mind, and appeals to higher authority were fruitless. She was therefore responsible for all trials and tribulations among mortals.

Left: The Lindisfarne Stone, from Northumbria, Britain, showing seven Viking warriors. It is believed that the carving commemorates the Viking attack on the Holy Island in around AD 793.

Above: A ninteenth-century book illustration showing Tyr, the bravest of all the gods. Note his amputated right hand, which was bitten off when he put it in the mouth of the wolf Fenris.

THOR: the son of Odin and Fjorgyn. Thor was associated with thunder, the sky, fertility and the law. Armed with his hammer, Miölnir, and the girdle of his strength, he had a simple way of righting wrongs: if it moves, kill it. The other gods – notably Loki – took advantage of Thor's simplicity on numerous occasions.

TYR: the god of war; son of Frigga by either Odin or the giant Hymir. He was generally regarded as the bravest of all the gods. When the Aesir were preparing to bind Fenris using the chain called Gleipnir, the giant wolf refused to submit unless one of the gods put his arm in the wolf's mouth as a guarantee. Tyr volunteered and, perhaps predictably, thereby lost his right hand.

ULL (HOLLER, OLLER, ULLER, VULDER): the god of winter, hunting, archery, death and skiing; a son of Sif, stepson of Thor and maybe husband of the giantess Skadi. Ull, possibly a lover of Frigga, was regarded as the next most important god after Odin but never attained great popularity because of the frigid season with which he was associated. Some versions of Norse mythology tell how each year, in the summer, Ull is forced to spend some months in Hel so that Odin, in his guise as the god of summer, can govern the weather. The Aurora Borealis was believed to be Ull putting on a visual display.

URD (URDR, WURD): one of the Norns.

Below right: A tenth-century Viking axe, inlaid with silver, from Mammen, Denmark.